For Jennifer, of course.

And for J.W.

*Our every anguish is answered by
the nearness of The Day.*

PREPARE THE WAY

DEVOTIONS FOR ADVENT

©2021 Rich Lambert

All rights reserved.

Published in Houston, Texas by Bible Study Media, Inc.
ISBN # 978-1-942243-49-6
Ebook ISBN # 978-1-942243-51-9

Library of Congress Control Number: 2021918794

No part of this publication may be reproduced, stored in retrieval system, or transmitted in any form or by any means electronic, mechanical, photocopy, recording, or otherwise except for brief quotations in printed reviews, without the prior written permission of the publisher.
www.biblestudymedia.com.

All Scripture quotations are from the ESV® Bible (The Holy Bible, English Standard Version®), copyright © 2001 by Crossway, a publishing ministry of Good News Publishers. Used by permission.
All rights reserved.

Printed in the United States of America.

How to Use This Book
A Note from the Author

This book is a map drawn up to help you settle into a seasonal place of residence, *Advent.* Maps give us a sense of direction and place, so we feel less like strangers and more like locals.

This map is built on four main highways into this new locale—the four Sundays of Advent along with the four weeks that trail after them. Each highway has four side streets that branch off from it—the four Scripture passages assigned to each Sunday according to the Revised Common Lectionary. These four Sunday readings are the subject and source of the daily devotionals for the week following, which creates a bit of a math problem. With four weekly Scripture passages and seven days to a week, there aren't enough passages to match the number of days. It's the old hot-dog-and-bun conundrum. So, for three of the days each week, a cul-de-sac is constructed out of a repeated text, where we look at a different aspect of the same text. If cul-de-sacs aren't to your taste, you can always drive past them and skip the detour altogether. If you do turn in, the nice thing about cul-de-sacs is, if you just follow them all the way around, eventually they bring you back out to the main road.

A few more thoughts on repetition. For some reason, modern readers feel cheated by it. They feel like they are being sold used goods instead of something new and unspoiled. That is a bias I think we should work hard to break, and here are just a few reasons why:

1. Every passage of Scripture is an ocean we could spend a lifetime exploring and still not discover it all. Repetition in Scripture reading is an act of diving deep and expecting to find new wonders floating just a little deeper than we were able to reach on previous dives.
2. Repetition is to Christian meditation what inhaling is to breathing. So, breathe deep.
3. Repetition is the lost tool of pedagogy. It is a refiner's tool.
4. If Scripture is spiritual food for the soul, chew slowly. Savor the feast.

How did we decide which passages to repeat? Author's choice. It was entirely arbitrary. For days that needed a borrowed text, I wrote about whatever I found in that week's readings that bothered or puzzled me, or about whatever seemed strange and out of place for some reason, or about what took my breath away, or what left me in tears. I read these verses over and over and over again, I wrung myself out in prayer, and then I tried to follow the Holy Spirit across the keyboard hoping to find what my heart needed most and trusting that your heart might need something very much the same.

Now that the map is in your hands, how you use it falls entirely to the discretion of the mapholder. You can walk and measure every square inch of this neighborhood like the town surveyor. You can amble and wander, routeless, like a dog-walker at the end of a long and costly day. You can visit the same site 28 days in a row and never make it from one end of this map to the other. It doesn't much matter, so long as you trust the Spirit of God to show you around the place, and you expect to find the Lamb of God himself around every corner. However you spend your time here, the goal is to make Advent feel less like a rest stop and more like home.

Rich Lambert

TABLE OF CONTENTS

09 INTRODUCTION:
Advent, Our Forgotten Relative

15 WEEK 1:
God Makes a Promise to Save and Keeps It in Jesus

32 WEEK 2:
God Sends Messengers to Point to Jesus as the Kept Promise of Salvation

50 WEEK 3:
Worship Is Rejoicing in the Promise of Jesus

66 WEEK 4:
The Promise Is Not Finished

Introduction:
Advent, Our Forgotten Relative
Four Reasons We Have Lost the Meaning and Celebration of Advent

Advent is like that distant relative who shows up throughout the family photo album, but whom no one can name or place correctly on the family tree. There he is, in glossy black and white, always with his dazzling, horsey grin and his thick blonde hair slicked back and to the side and tucked behind protruding ears, always with each arm thrown over the shoulders of a cousin, and no one can agree exactly where he fits in the lineage. Some family members even begin to suspect that he's no relation at all, just a neighbor kid who happened to turn up every time the camera came out. Come late November and most of December, *Advent* is all the talk, but no one is quite sure what we mean by it. *Advent, Advent, Advent,* and we smile and nod as if we understand full well, but we don't really have a clue what it is or how it fits.

The one thing we *can* say, if pressed, is that *advent* means arrival, and we are fairly certain that it has something to do with the arrival of Jesus. Not sure what to say beyond that, we make Advent a kind of second Lent, a season of preparation. In the same way that Lent is a prelude of repentance and denial on the way to the hallelujahs of Easter, we think that Advent must be a season of darkness and austerity as we await the "Joy to the World" of Messiah's birth. From there we do the only thing we can think to do to prepare—we count down the days, 25 of them in all. We have specially made calendars for the occasion, most of them thin cardboard boxes with perforated, numbered doors that dispense all kinds of things that don't seem to have any connection at all to the coming of Jesus—Lego toys, mini bottles of liquor, molded chocolates wrapped in foil. Advent is now a word that means, *not quite Christmas*, an appetizer before the feast, a teaser before the blockbuster, a ramp-up to the main event. The reason we barely recognize Advent any longer is, we've attached it to the wrong main event. It is not the first arrival of Jesus that Advent looks toward, but his second. It is not his appearing in a manger that Advent signifies; it is his returning on the clouds. Advent is a buzzing, crackling neon sign that points past the nativity of Jesus to the end of the age at his second coming. Advent for the Christian church has always meant the joyous arrival of the end. So how have we forgotten so completely? As with every case of forgetting, our forgetting of Advent happened gradually and in stages.

We have forgotten the meaning of Advent because of its place on the calendar. Actually, Advent is a tangle of two calendars. The span of five-ish weeks stretching from the last days of November across the entire month of December marks the end of the Gregorian calendar, but it is the start of the ecclesiastical calendar. The new church year begins with the first Sunday of Advent (the final Sunday of November)[1], just as the annual calendar is winding to a close. What's confounding about this is that we begin the church year with a season of looking for the world to end! What sense does it make to start with the end?! It makes little sense if we are marking chronology and time, but it makes perfect sense if we are marking theological importance. By kicking off the new church year with a five-week season that anticipates the end of the ages, the church is confessing, *We have many hopes for God's blessing this year, but the greatest blessing of all would be for Jesus to come back! By far, the best thing that could happen this year is the second coming of Christ!* So the church begins a new cycle of its calendar by celebrating its greatest hope! That hope, however, is easily blurred in the clash of dueling calendars.

We have forgotten the meaning of Advent because we have confused its relation to Christmas. Advent sits too close to Christmas for its own good. Because they are such close neighbors, we reason, the one must lead into the other. Not quite. In fact, to properly understand the relationship of Advent to Christmas, we need to flip their importance.

---

[1] *Technically, Advent begins on All Souls Day, November 1st, but due to the sprawl of major national holidays (Halloween and Thanksgiving), much of the American church defers the start of the Advent season to the last Sunday in November.*

Instead of Advent building our hope toward Christmas, Christmas assures us that the promise of Advent is not just a wild wish. Christmas is a consolation prize. If another Advent passes without the return of Christ, we still have the celebration that Jesus was born into our world as the initiation of redemption to tide us over until next Advent! But together the two are like cousins of promise—each promise amplifies the other. The promise of Christmas is that redemption has come; the promise of Advent is that redemption is *still* coming and will be completed soon, however long that may be. Christmas is Advent's guarantee; if God kept his promise to send us salvation in the birth of Jesus, it's a sure bet that God will keep the remainder of that promise and send Jesus again to complete salvation through re-creation!

We have forgotten the meaning of Advent because it is a fast and not a feast. Christmas is a feast. It is about *material joys* and *more*. We load ourselves down at Christmas with all kinds of trinkets that promise to keep us happy through the coming year and beyond. Advent is the opposite. It is about *spiritual joys* and *less*. Advent is a dislodging of ourselves, a turning loose of this world as we turn toward the world to come. Admittedly, it's hard to get excited about a season of fasting with a festival of fullness just around the corner! It's also a problem that so many Advents have come and gone, and here we are celebrating another one. Jesus has stayed away for so long, some of us, maybe most of us, are doubtful that he'll return. Of course we are half-hearted about Advent. Nothing much ever comes of it, but Christmas we can count on! Christmas is reliable, and Advent has yet to deliver. But the New Testament saints, who watched Jesus rise to heaven in a cloud, were constantly searching the skies for his return. They walked around with cricks in their necks, they were so eager for it. The second to the last verse of the Bible has Jesus saying, *"Surely I am coming soon,"* and the saints respond in the same verse, *"Amen. Come, Lord Jesus!"* (Rev. 22:20).

We should add that to our liturgical practice. Instead of closing our prayers with a mumbled "Amen," we should drag up the urgency of Advent in the conclusion to all our prayers the way saints used to do it—"Amen. Come, Lord Jesus!" AND, we should recover that nagging sense of soon. We should develop cricks in our necks again from looking up too much.

We have forgotten the meaning of Advent because Advent is a disposition, not a day. It is actually a way of relating to the world. It is a way of moving and conducting ourselves in hopeful certainty. If Jesus is coming back, we have something to say to the world. If Jesus is coming back, we have a purposeful way of ministering to those in need. If Jesus is coming back, then we can wipe away tears with assurance, and laugh with abandon, and oppose evil with confidence. If Jesus is coming back, we can offer up full-throated worship. If Jesus is coming back, none of our days should ever fall flat, or be over-inflated, again. Advent was never intended to be confined to a corner of the calendar. For the Christian, every day is Advent, an extension of Passover for the end of days. We go to bed with our shoes on our feet and our coats fastened around us, walking sticks tucked under our arms. We are ready to be called away in an instant, and we live by the mindset that each day our feet hit the floor could be our last in this place, God willing. Every day we are ready to leave and while we wait, by grace, we do all we can to get others ready to travel with us.

Advent has become the unidentified relative in our family album because after a while, it was just easier to forget than to remember. In our amnesia, we treat it as a yawning preamble to Christmas, but in truth it is the most important season on the church calendar. Every other Christian season and holiday commemorates what God has already done. Advent is the only celebration that reaches for what God has yet to do. That makes it alive and electric, buzzing with charged anticipation and surprise. Advent isn't so much a whisper from the next room as the London Philharmonic arranged at the foot of your bed as you sleep, awaiting the first downstroke from the conductor's baton. It is not a flickering candle-glow in the window, it is the orange laughter of dawn vaulting over the dark wall at the horizon and outrunning the night guards. It is not slouching on the platform while waiting on a late commuter train, it is sitting bolt upright on the edge of your seat and ready to be yanked clean out of it. It is like the emcee stepping to the front of the stage to announce with the sweep of an arm, "And now the moment you've all been waiting for," just as the curtain lifts and the audience gasps and erupts into wild and endless applause. Advent has always lived on the razor edge of holy impatience for saints and disciples—their, "How long, O Lord?" With each passing year, may your wait grow joyfully harder. Happy Advent.

WEEK 1
God Makes a Promise to Save and Keeps It in Jesus

Jeremiah 33:14-16; Psalm 25:1-9; 1 Thessalonians 3:9-13; Luke 21:25-36

Day 1 - Jeremiah 33:14-16
The Long Promise

Christianity is one long promise that stretches through the ages. Christians are those who wait for that long promise to be kept. Here again in these verses, God is reciting the promise he made in the hearing of those to whom he made it.

Many of us have made promises and tried to slip free of them at one time or another. But God does something peculiar with the promises he makes. He keeps proclaiming them in public and holding himself to them. He has never welched on even the slightest edge of his promise to save sinners, and so it is not an insult for God to be reminded of his promise. Because his promise is his glory, he loves to recite it in public. It is a way of saying, "No one has ever made promises like this, and no one has ever kept promises like this, either. But I have, and will, and am…" Because his promises are our glory, too, we should join in the full-throated, lusty recitation of them. We should call on him to remember his long promise and not be slow in fulfilling it, as a way of pledging that we have not forgotten either.

We are uncomfortable with language like this. It feels presumptuous, and pushy, improper even, to speak so boldly. The Bible says otherwise. Because he is true to his word eternally, he does not blush when we repeat it back to him. Bold cries to the Lord to do what he swore in the garden, what he initiated in the manger, what he completed in the crucifixion and resurrection and ascension, and what he will fulfill in Messiah's triumphant return is not arrogant talk from brash tongues. It is the language of humility and faith. It is the language of a people who hold a long promise in their hearts, and hold their breath to see it done. When we exhale, it will sound like "Hallelujah!"

Faith and Practice: Use these verses to write out a prayer calling upon God to keep his long promise in the return of Messiah. Notice how bold the words of the verses are. See if you can use that same boldness in crafting your own prayer.

Day 2 - Jeremiah 33:14-16
The Promise Is a Person

The great promise of God is a person, not a theological abstraction. Theology has its place, of course, but the whole purpose of theology is to lay out for us the beautiful profile and portrait of a person. All of this is a tremendous relief because in various ways we have made a bloody mess of God's promise. We reduce it to some divine secret that taunts and teases us as it plays just out of our reach, a kind of theological leprechaun running through the hills, evading and eluding, demanding capture and haggling before reluctantly turning loose the pot of gold. Or think of the countless sermons that present the promise of God as an incantation—if we could only puzzle out the *right* words, and then say those *right* words in just the *right* way, the gates of heaven would open for us. All wrong. Jeremiah, the bad news prophet, says the great promise of God is not an "it" to be captured and bested, but a "he" with good news on his mind. The shock of Jeremiah's prophecy is that it reverses the weight and force of the promise as we understand it, or *mis*understand it to be more to the point—instead of *us* pursuing the promise, *he* does all the pursuing.

"Righteousness himself is coming," Jeremiah forecasts, "and you can't miss him because he's coming from the house of David. AND you'll know him by this name, 'The Lord is our righteousness.'" (See v. 15, 16.) What this means on the street level is that the promise is not coming to shame us. The promise is coming to relieve our shame by making himself the only approval we will ever need to wear. From the manger he spilled into, to the cross he was nailed upon, to the tomb he cartwheeled out of, his righteousness was unfailing, and so when we wear his righteousness, nothing else will ever fit us quite right again—not fear, not guilt, not self-loathing and condemnation, not our frantic and feverish tidying ourselves up, not our brazen self-promotion. The promise is not coming to catch us in our failure to measure up; he comes to be our full measure. Repentance then is simply trading our clothes for his. That means, of course, that our experience of this world can be much more joyful than we often make it. It also means that our welcome of the next world can be joyful, too. For us, the return of Jesus does not feel like a trap we can't escape, it feels like an embrace we never want to leave.

Faith and Practice: How could wearing the righteousness of Jesus as your only righteousness set you free and fill you with joy today?

Day 3 - Psalm 25:1-9
Waiting Hurts

This prayer is a provocation. "If my enemies humiliate me, O Lord, they also humiliate you. If they triumph over me, they triumph over you. If I am put to shame, you share in that shame." (See verses 2-3.) What confuses and discomforts Christians about this kind of provoking prayer is that we wonder how David could say such a thing, and to God no less! Actually, David is not saying this at all. Rather, David is saying, "This is what your enemies will say! You have been away too long, and they say you will not return! You're not going to let them get away with this are you? You won't let them be proven right about you, will you?"

Jesus is God's resounding answer to this wrenching worry. Jesus has put every particular shame to shame with his cross. Jesus has humiliated every version of death we have settled for in his resurrection. Jesus has mocked every enemy of faith and righteousness with the victor's homecoming in his ascension. His second coming will be an eternal gloating over them all. It will feel like a goodness long overdue, but delivered in full, and then some! It will feel like a wildly hilarious vindication—like belly laughing, "We were right to trust in you! We were right to lift our souls to you! We were not put to shame!"

Then why has he stayed away so long? He has stayed away so long to shame our shame even further, to humiliate our humiliation even more, to frustrate the treacherous completely. He leads them to believe they are winning only to show in his appearing that they were never truly winning at all. The pain and anxiety of our waiting only deepens our satisfaction. The pain of it makes his coming more urgent, the stakes more desperate, and our celebration more ultimate. In the meantime, David shows us how to pray our pain, "You won't let them win, will you?" In answer, the manger, the cross, and the empty tomb all echo their chorus of reassurance.

Faith and Practice: Which are you more likely to do when in pain and distress? Grumble internally, complain to another person, pray prayers of provocation? Do you need to change your habit, and what would that change of habit bring?

Day 4 - Psalm 25:1-9
Waiting Is Active

Expectant waiting is active waiting. When we are expecting the birth of a child, we spend months converting the spare room into a nursery. As the wedding day approaches, a dress is bought, venues secured, invitations mailed, and RSVPs collected. As we count down to December 25, shopping lists are crossed off, a tree is set up and lit, menus are planned, and travel arranged. The only waiting done passively is the waiting of dread.

Characteristically, the psalmist is waiting for salvation—salvation from enemies, and from the shame and humiliation these enemies wield. While he waits, the psalmist walks in God's "paths" (v. 4). These

paths are where God himself walks, and so they are the places where God is sure to be found. The paths are all clearly marked and worn with holy traffic: repentance that brings release and relief (v. 6, 7), surrendered and trusting obedience (v. 8), believing that God has a sure and looming salvation that is more than worth the agonizing wait (v. 5), keeping covenant by bringing our need and weakness to be answered with his joyous strength and merry mercy (v. 10), keeping his testimonies as the only reliable stories we have to live by (v. 10), and humility as the way of wisdom (v. 9). The psalm reads like a user's manual for active waiting, and as we walk these paths with the psalmist, we are waiting for salvation with him, which is to say, we are walking toward our salvation. We are walking out to meet Jesus at his return.

We shouldn't make the mistake of thinking we are the only ones actively waiting, though. The enemies are scheming, the psalmist says. They keep busy laying up plans and laying out traps. They lie in ambush because they would love nothing more than to chase us from the paths, so we will have to run their gauntlet of insults, blasphemies, and threats. As we walk on, we will have to remember and remind one another that active waiting means also brushing right past them. If the dragon could not devour Jesus in the manger (Rev. 12:4), if the deceiver could not tempt him away from the cross (Matthew 4:1-11), if death failed to seal him away in the tomb (John 20:1-10), then nothing will obstruct his second coming, and in turn nothing can slow our waiting strides. One thing is certain in all this waiting, we cannot be kept from Jesus because he will not be kept from us. Here is another certainty according to the psalmist, because Jesus cannot be disappointed at his own goodness (v. 7), we won't be disappointed with it either (v. 8), and every last enemy will be swept away by it when Jesus brings it trailing behind him in a gracious wake (v. 3).

Faith and Practice: What does active waiting look like for you today?

Day 5 - 1 Thessalonians 3:9-13
Waiting Is Abounding

St. Paul's desire for the Thessalonians is an overwhelming desire with very little personal stake. Paul did not live in covenant faithfulness for them, he didn't die for them as a sin atonement, he didn't rise for them as eternal vindication, so the love and desire he has for them is a transplanted love and desire; it is donated, loaned, shared at best. The love and desire Paul feels for the Thessalonian saints is the love and desire Jesus has for them reaching *through* Paul.

Paul's earnest prayers for them are extensions of Jesus's own intercessions; Paul's longing to see them face to face is rooted in Jesus's own unnegotiable bodily return; Paul's longing to restore what is lacking in Thessalonian faith is Jesus's promise to turn faith to sight. If Paul wanted to be with the Thessalonians, Jesus wants to be with us more. To Jesus, you are not an obligation, or an inconvenience. To Jesus, you are his joy and desire through the ages.

What is it that propels this longing of Jesus, and "directs his way to us" (v. 11)? It is the joy that Jesus has for the work he has done in you (v. 9). It is the joy he has for your sakes before God, meaning it is the joy he has for his resemblance grown and harvested in you. It is the joy he has for the re-creation he has begun in you and will bring to completion at his return (v. 13). After all, the joy of the harvest is not for the fruit, not for the tree, but for the owner of the orchard.

In the meantime, as we wait for the appointed and eternal day, St. Paul advises us to sample this joy, like kids scooping fingers full of frosting out of a cake. His word for it is more elegant, but the sentiment is the same. Paul says, we should *abound* while we wait (v. 12). We are to fill ourselves up to overflowing with those qualities of Jesus we love most, the ones he has planted in us to be shared and enjoyed with him.

Abound in love, the real kind, the kind Jesus displayed—demanding and sacrificial and graciously withholding nothing.

Abound in holiness, not the glue and paper merit badges we fashion for ourselves with performative piety, but the sort that is a Christ-resemblant beauty, the kind that resists the vandalism and mutilation and marring done by sin.

Abound in thanksgiving, not the airy, helium-filled sentiments we casually float around, but the kind of thanksgiving that marks and celebrates every single grace visited upon us, the kind that collects these graces, and shows them off, the kind that enthusiastically helps others build their own collections.

Abound while you wait, St. Paul counsels, and you will feel the gravitational joy, desire, and longing Jesus has for you.

Faith and Practice: What will you abound in today?

Day 6 - Luke 21:25-36

Start Early

It's not as if you can miss out on the Day of Jesus's return. That is not the heart of this warning at all! In fact, none of us will miss it according to the account: *"For it will come upon all who dwell on the face of the whole earth"* (v. 35). And it's not as if Christ-lovers can accidentally find themselves stranded on the wrong side of the Day, swept up in the judgment and mistaken for goats rather than recognized as sheep (Matthew 25:34), although many Christians have a self-condemning tendency to read it this way.

In the passage, Jesus is addressing a customarily mixed crowd of disciples and detractors. Much of his tirade is aimed at those in the audience with their arms crossed, their heads cocked sideways, and their eyes narrowed to slits. He's railing against disbelievers and discreditors, and yet there is still a heavy warning for his band of followers. What we are warned against in the closing verses of this passage is not the judgment, but missing out on the joy of the Day! Specifically, we are warned against becoming numb while we wait (v. 34). We are warned about distracting ourselves with empty frivolities and the *"cares of this life"*—shorthand for "things that won't last." For those who have ears to hear, Jesus is saying that he is making us full beneficiaries of an incontestable estate, so we can stop weighing ourselves down by filling our pockets with things that are already passing away (v. 34). We are warned to stay awake, and not sleep through the fanfare of the Day because we have hijacked ourselves with far lesser concerns that aren't even worth the paper we draw them up and notarize them on. To sum all of it up, we are warned not to lull ourselves into thinking that the Day is not coming.

We already know the truth of these verses, even if we get tangled in the words a bit—the buildup is almost as good as the Day itself! Or at the very least, the buildup adds to the Day! Much of the fun in Christmas is the aching anticipation as the day inches closer. It is the pleading wish we send up every time we exclaim, "I can't wait!" In the same way, is there a scene more tragic than yawning ourselves awake late in the day on December 25th and asking, "What is today's date?" A day that sneaks up on you is a day that's sneaked past, especially if it's deserving of all the hoopla!

Disciples caught unready when the Day arrives won't be punished with the judgment of rejection. The trap Jesus speaks of in verse 34 is a hazard only for the hardened denier. What Jesus warns us against is missing out on the giddy hope of our coming inheritance! At the start of this chapter, Jesus praises a widow for throwing her last coppers in the temple coffers (Luke 21:1-4). Later in the chapter, when we arrive at today's verses, he is exhorting us to look for the Day with that same kind of impoverished faith, that same kind of desperate emptiness that exclaims with full conviction, "I give my less-than-nothing for your way-beyond-more!" If we do, Jesus says, then ours is an empty fullness: "For many, the Day will come like sands running out, but for you, the Day arrives like your ship coming in! So what are you waiting for? Down to the shoreline! Up to the cliffs! Out on the docks! Strain at the horizon! It won't be long..."

There is a lot of celebration and electricity in the anticipation of our festival days! Jesus is giving us permission to start celebrating early. Really, he is inviting us to be like that family on the block who, without even a hint of embarrassment, leave their Christmas lights up year-round.

Faith and Practice: What in your life (behaviors, practices, activities, dispositions) are mini-celebrations and previews of the return of Jesus? What in your life are like Christmas lights left up too long, illuminating the Day of Jesus's coming? Or maybe, do you need to hang up a few more strands?

Day 7 - Luke 21:25-36

You Are Signs

Jesus says the day of his coming should come as no surprise. The signs are all around us that the Day is near. The heavens and earth cry out steadily *for* the return of Jesus, not suddenly *at* his return. The heavens tumble from their vault and the seas spill from their basins because they convulse and retch with the torments of sin and the fall. Even the creation is longing and groaning and pleading for redemption at the return of Jesus. We sing of these same signs each December as we belt out *Joy to the World*: "No more let sins and sorrows grow, nor thorns infest the ground. He comes to make his blessings flow, far as the curse is found." When Jesus returns, the curse is shattered and the pains of sin will be relieved for all the creation, and nature will sing the fanfare at his victory parade just as loudly as the disciples who line the route, if the old carol is to be believed.

Admittedly, it feels out of place to sing *Joy to the World* while the sky is falling and the earth is heaving. Not everyone has eyes of faith to see these cataclysms as sin's grip slipping from our world. To help us along, Jesus sends a shaft of sunlight straight through the heart of this text that reads predominantly like storm clouds of sorrow and gloom. In the middle of this passage, Jesus tells a parable (v. 29-32) in which he makes two startling claims.

The first claim is, if you read the signs correctly, you can tell which season we are in, and by all indications it's almost... *SUMMER* (v. 30)! Can you believe it?! Not the bleak scarcity of winter, but the lush, ripe, hothouse of summer.

The second claim is even more shocking than the first. *You* are the good news signs that summer is coming. *You* are the sprouting leaves on the trees (v. 30). *You* are the fig tree about to throw its fruit (v. 29)! You are mysteriously and simultaneously rooted in the Son and reaching for him. You are mysteriously and simultaneously bearing fruit *from* him and *for* him. You stand as living signs that salvation and grace invaded our world using a manger for his chariot. You stand as living, breathing, growing, towering signs that Jesus is returning to set up his full government of redemption and repave and replant every square inch of this place with love and glory. That means also that every gluttonous inequity, exploitation, violence, and abuse will be uprooted, cut down, weeded, and burned while we stand by and sing, *"Repeat the sounding joy, repeat the sounding joy, repeat, repeat the sounding joy!"*

We aren't quite there yet, though. For now, you are to keep pushing your way to leaf and fruit. Every time you give up on your own efforts and make yourself dependent on what Jesus has accomplished; every time you give up on your wisdom and make the words and mind of Christ your knowing; every time you mute your sovereignty and magnify his, you blossom and bloom. You call the nations out of their wailing distress and perplexity (v. 25). You call your neighbors out of fainting and fear (v. 26). You invite them to give up their hand wringing and doomsaying and join our singing. The mystery of this passage is that you are an orchard planted in an apocalypse. So, stand tall (v. 28). Lift your head. Bear the fruit of faith in Jesus the Son of God. Sing with all your might, *"Summer is coming!"*

Faith and Practice: Today, practice the redemptive hope of *Joy to the World!* Find an infestation of thorns, a place where the curse seems to have a strong hold, and be present as a living sign of Christ's blessing. In Christ, you are an eviction notice to sin and death.

WEEK 2
God Sends Messengers to Point to Jesus as the Kept Promise of Salvation

Malachi 3:1-4; Luke 1:68-79; Philippians 1:3-11; Luke 3:1-6

Day 8 - Malachi 3:1-4

Fire and Soap

Who can stand before Jesus when he appears? Only those who have been touched, healed, purified by him. Only those whom he has changed to present to himself as a worthy offering.

This means, of course, that we possess a deep-seated knowledge that we are unworthy in ourselves. The prophecy tells us that Jesus is like a refiner's fire. Living in Jesus means that by his mere presence our impurities and contaminants and unholiness are burned away. They are cooked off. They cannot remain in us, because they are not welcome in him. That is good news, even if the process itself is

painful at points. The prophecy also says that Jesus is like a fuller's soap; a fuller's job was to beat or stomp soap deep into the fibers of sheep's wool so that dirt and oil could be stripped from it, and a whitened cloth could be produced. Living in Jesus means his joyful righteousness and faithfulness are like

an astringent that bleaches out of us not just the guilt of sin, but also the delusion that we can keep our sin close without being devoured by it. It dissolves the notion that we can manage and control our sin when in reality it manages and controls us. This leaching of sin-toxins brings discomfort, but eventually the sin itself becomes the discomfort. Living by repentance and faith at the foot of Jesus's cross and in the mouth of his empty tomb, our impurities and wrongs, and eventually the cravings and shame of them too, are smelted and scrubbed away. This is no empty appraisal. Having been justified in his sacrifice, being sanctified through his Spirit, set aside to be glorified at his return, we are also being changed in quality to match his. The essence of who he is transforms the essence of who we are.

We do not fear the day of judgment because refinement is our judgment. It is a judgment of being revalued, not rejected. It is the acknowledged judgment of having lost our original worth, and being gladly reforged in his. All who feel and know their own lacking worth can be presented in him as fully pleasing offerings and stand unflinching and unhidden at his coming.

This makes us an army of bold and free messengers. Our message? We all start off as hunks of cheap alloy and stained fleeces but we don't all end up that way. Then again, no slab of alloy ever spun itself to pure gold, nor has sooty wool ever dyed itself Wimbledon white. The cross and empty tomb are all the fire and soap we need.

Faith and Practice: How is he refining you right now? Give thanks for even the discomfort and pain of it. His beauty, worked in you, is eternal beauty.

Day 9 - Luke 1:68-79

Unmuted Messengers

What a turnaround for old Zechariah. Just nine months earlier, he had been all doubt and disbelief when the angel appeared before him while serving priestly duty in the temple. That was Zechariah's big mistake, by the way. While burning incense, the symbol of the prayers of God's people wafting to heaven and being inhaled by God as sweet fragrant perfume, an angel stands in front of Zechariah and says, "Peace be with you, old man. God has answered *your* prayers, and those of *your* wife Elizabeth. You're going to be a father!" And Zecha-

riah responds, "Oh, come on!" Zechariah's sin of unbelief is not uncommon to many of us. We believe God answers prayers, just not *our* prayers. We believe God is good, just not so good to *us*.

So to help Zechariah out, to help the crusty old priest believe again that God does in fact hear and answer prayer, the angel struck him dumb. For nine months Zechariah could do nothing but pray. It did the trick. Now, when God un-cements Zechariah's vocal cords, Zechariah is all prophecy and promise. Part of what he unleashes is God's commissioning of his infant son (v. 76-77). But the story here is not John, who will grow up to be Messiah's prophet one day. At this point in our family story, John is just a squalling pink bundle, so we will have to wait on John. The story here is Zechariah, who *is* Messiah's prophet *today*. That is the Gospel if ever we've witnessed it: every trophy of grace was once a lost cause and a miserable failure. His leaden tongue now loose and free, Zechariah blazes like a prophetic wildfire.

The major theme of Zechariah's prophecy is *freedom*: Blessed be the Lord who has come to set his people *free*; to set us free from the hands of our enemies; *free* to worship him without fear. Zechariah is an eloquent messenger of this God-given freedom because he had been set free from his doubt and denial, and dumbness as a result of them.

You don't have to argue with an angel to be struck dumb. For most of us, dumbness is voluntary. We *believe* in God, we *need* his promise of salvation, but we've found worldly ways to cope during the long seasons of waiting, and so we keep the observances of worship and faith religiously, but robotically. We go to prayers, mumble confessions of sin, kneel for the eucharist, renounce Satan at the baptismal font, but we don't expect much to come of it, not in our lifetimes anyway. And then Jesus meets one of us in the pew, on the kneeling bench, at the altar rail, or at the kitchen table over coffee and an open Bible or prayer book one morning. And suddenly, he convinces us he *is* God's compassion to us. He convinces us he *is* the headwaters of eternal light (the "Dawnspring") shining through our settled darkness and the shadows of death we've made home. He persuades us that he *is* the knowledge of salvation, he is our forgiveness of sins. He *is* our full freedom. He *is* our message and our boldness. And our tongues are cut loose from their voluntary shackles. Jesus gives himself another Zechariah, a passive saint transformed into a powder keg prophet.

God's Gospel of salvation and grace is such good news, he sends messengers to march out before it in a rollicking procession. The God who specializes in unlikely births knows just how to conceive, gestate, and deliver his messengers to lead the world in rejoicing. There were two messengers born on this day. For now anyway, John is the least interesting of the two. That's the story here; John has his treasured place in our family narrative, but Jesus has an army of Zechariahs.

Faith and Practice: Be specific. What is the cause of your voluntary dumbness? If you are brave enough, confess it without fear, and ask him to cut loose your tongue to spread the joyful good news.

Day 10 - Malachi 3:1-4 and Luke 1:68-79

Prepare the Way

Just because God sends messengers to *prepare the way* doesn't mean everyone will be glad to hear about it. *Prepare the way* means prepare the people to receive the Coming One. It is a message of inconvenience because it is a message of reordering our lives. Remember, the message is the Coming One is a refiner's fire and fuller's soap. To be prepared for him means to be transformed for him. It is an equation of holy discomfort.

In Zechariah's song, he crows out long, history-soaked verses that his baby boy will grow to be a forerunner announcing that the One who comes after him is the Promise—the Promise from the House of David, the Promise of the holy covenant, the Promise sworn to Abraham with a flint knife and a fire pot; that doesn't mean, though, that folks are still holding their breath waiting on this Promise. Many have made promises to themselves, promises that sound like, "I'm gonna get what's coming to me," or "I'm going to take what's mine," or "Who says you can't have it all?"

John the forerunner ran into an immovable opponent during his mission of preparation. He was out in the wilderness, dressed in furs and skins, eating wild honey with insect legs stuck in his teeth, preaching a baptism of repentance. John's entire life was a signpost that the things of this world aren't really the important things after all. John's word for this was "Repent!", and he yelled out the word repeatedly as he waded out into the Jordan River and poured water over people to show that when Messiah finally showed up he would have to wash us all if we were to have anything to do with him.

Crowds flocked to size up John and his message, but he ran afoul of the puppet king. This king, Herod, was a picture of success, by ancient and modern standards, and he was willing to do whatever it takes to get ahead. John in the meantime stood waist deep in the river on the outskirts of town yelling at anyone who would listen, that that sort of track record might be impressive to power brokers and toadies, but two people who weren't impressed were the righteous God of Israel, and his Coming One. So if the king and his court knew what was good for them, they'd better repent and be washed, too. It got under the king's skin to be sure. It also got John a stint in the king's dungeon, and later a silver platter for his head. But just before John was dispatched, while he was languishing in his cell, he sent his disciples to find Jesus and ask him a question: "Are you really the Promised One? Are you the One we are to receive? Are you the One keeping score, and the One who will settle the score, too? Tell me I haven't made a terrible mistake."

Jesus sent John's disciples back with the message that the blind were ditching their dark glasses and tin cups, the lame were dancing in the streets, formerly unclean lepers were handing out bear-hugs, the deaf had laughter ringing in their ears, the dead weren't dead anymore and were selling their grave plots at bargain basement prices, and the poor were hearing the news that to be poor in this life is to be rich in the next. In other words, everything John had preached was already coming true. In that exchange, John was no longer just a messenger, he was a man most in need of the message.

Just because there are people who oppose the message doesn't mean there aren't plenty of others dying to hear it. And who are those who will hear and receive? The ones Zechariah sang about at the birth of his baby boy, long before the river washings, the preaching circuits, the dungeon, and the platter. Those who will hear are those who long to be *free—free from sin, free from guilt, free from fear, free from striving and never measuring up, free from making their own way and looking out for number one, free from making excuses and lying to themselves, free from the exhaustion of self-sufficiency, free from the treasures of this world that aren't nearly treasure enough.* God has a message of good news, so he sends good news messengers to prepare the way for the Promised One, who will return like a victor shoveling out spoils. There are always those who oppose this message, but there are also always those desperate to hear and receive it. These are the ones John and Zechariah, and the rest of us, are sent to prepare.

Faith and Practice: Do you know anyone longing to be free? Are you willing to carry to them the message?

Day 11 - Philippians 1:3-11

Conspiracy for Reconciliation

The Gospel is not private. Most things in our world have been reduced to the language of privatized possession and ownership, so perhaps it shouldn't surprise us that we unconsciously do the same with our participation in the Gospel: *my* church, *my* faith, *my* heart, *my* quiet time, *my* ministry, *my* spiritual gifts and passions. This is not the way St. Paul and the first Christians thought of it. They understood the Gospel to be our identity, which means we belong to it, and not the other way around. We are subject to it, not the other way around. We fit into it; we do not fit it into our lives. We are being made in the image of the Gospel of God in Jesus Christ; we are not authorized to make the Gospel in our image.

This sense of Gospel identity bleeds through Paul's letter to the Philippians. Paul reminds them that the work, the fruit, even the costs of the Gospel (which Paul calls graces! See v. 7.) are known not just to him, but also to the Philippians with him. However the translations choose to name it—partnership, sharing, partakers with me in grace, Paul's argument here is simple. Christ Jesus has done this work in Paul and in the Philippian Christians, and so Christ Jesus has given them the same work to do in the world for his name's sake. Together, they are enlisted, and us with them, in a holy conspiracy, an uprising of grace. The Gospel is a rival kingdom to every worldly power and system. To everything in our lives—education, business and finance, activism, conservation, farming, manufacturing, technology, politics, fitness and diet, medicine, psychology, shopping and consumption, career, and leisure—the Gospel says, "Yes, but no." There is not a single element in our world that doesn't need Gospel revision as the promise and preview that a new, sin-eradicated world is coming.

But to turn the world upside down by grace, it takes a colony of people serving an otherworldly kingdom in the heart of enemy territory. Paul and the Philippians call that colony by its more familiar names: *church* and *us*. The way Paul says it to the Philippians, the transformation that Jesus is working in all of them (v. 6) is supposed to spill out of them and into the world they engage in his name (v. 7, 9, 10). Imagine, just imagine how different the world might be if church wasn't just a series of voluntary meetings spread across the week, but it was a conscious Gospel renovation of everything that is broken and gluttonous in our world. What if, instead of greeting one another on Sunday, we rolled up our sleeves and linked arms all week? What if instead of bowing and quickly signing ourselves with the cross so no one can see, our collective faithful presence was a sign of the cross made over our surroundings? What injustices might be undone? What abuses might be healed? What corruptions might be evicted? What light might be spread? What hope might be restored, or newborn? What worship might be stirred and lifted up? Do you think it's even possible? Do you think the church can ever find its way back to her true identity as conspirators of reconciliation in the teeth of the kingdoms of fallenness and self? One thing's for sure, if the church ever *does* find its way to its true calling again, it will draw a lot of attention. Many neighbors will bang on the church doors to be let in. Many others will bang on the church doors with torches and pitchforks and warrants for our arrest. Either way, says St. Paul, the Gospel is a smashing success (v. 7)!

Faith and Practice: 1) How would our relationship to the Gospel and church shift if we stopped using the possessive pronoun "my" to talk about our participation in both? 2) How would cities, communities, and institutions change if Christians stopped thinking of themselves as individual operators, and began to think of themselves as reconciliation units and teams?

Day 12 - Luke 3:1-6
Wilderness

To any sharp-eyed observer, John was off his prophetic nut. Any respectable prophet knows you take the message to where the people are—maybe a soap box or a sandwich board at the busiest intersection in town during rush hour. For John's prophetic debut, he splashed around on the banks of the Jordan River, preaching hellfire and brimstone to no one in particular and dunking anyone who was bold enough to wander out to find him. A career-minded prophet might take to the late-night cable news-talk circuit, or set up a channel on YouTube and keep track of analytics; John set up shop in the wilderness. Wilderness is the opposite of Eden. Wilderness is the garden uprooted, the garden tossed, the garden lost and in ruins. If the garden was the setting for humanity in innocence, the wilderness is the setting for humanity after the fall[2]. It is a slide back toward the chaotic, roiling nothing that existed before God's good creation. That explains why John chooses this as the site for his tentless tent revivals. It also explains why just before John began his preaching campaign, Jesus came out here to be tempted.

When Jesus is tempted in the wilderness, Satan has home-field advantage. When Jesus withstands temptation with his righteous strength, Satan is defeated on his home turf. This in itself is good news! Sin overturned the garden, now grace has come to overturn the wilds. This 40-day heavyweight championship bout between the Son and the devil was an enacted preview of Jesus's later parable about tying up the strongman and robbing him blind while he watched (Luke 11:20-22). John continued this same theme, of course, with his riverside ministry.

John preached, "Salvation is coming and nothing can stop it! In fact, God says build a super highway right through the barrens—that means cut down the mountains, fill in the valleys and canyons, carve

---

2 *The city can be thought of as a wilderness with infrastructure.*

down the curves. Flat and straight is how he wants it, because his grace is coming like a bullet train, and nothing can stop him from reaching you, beloved!" That's the thing about John; he might have

been sun-scorched and Spirit-singed, but he burned with God's desire for sinners. So when he preached "Repent!" and "Be washed!", wiping the sweat from his eyes with the Jordan dripping from the hem of his garment, he was really proclaiming, "The Savior will cut back the wilderness of sin in you. He will chop out the hedgerows and burn them off, and he will plant and weed and cultivate and irrigate you until you produce fruit that is out of this world!" By the time John was done, his holy tirade could turn a box of snakes into a congregation of sons and daughters.

John is long since gone from this world, but his message echoes behind him. He is still the voice crying in the wilderness, and crying against our wilderness. The wilds in us are still being replanted as a garden, and the untamed places are losing real estate as the full redemption of Jesus draws near. Grace is still coming. Like a bullet train.

Faith and Practice: 1) What wild place in you has been replanted as a garden that belongs now to Jesus? Being specific in your answer will increase your rejoicing! 2) Does noticing particular sanctification and areas of growth in your life make you long for the coming of Jesus more?

Day 13 - Luke 3:1-6
Wilderness, Part 2

Location, location, location. It's the first rule of both real estate and prophecy. Place matters. Place *is* the message. If you wanted to find John, you had to make a day of it. Wear comfortable shoes and breathable clothing. Pack a lunch and bring an extra thermos of water. And a walking stick probably wouldn't hurt, either. Where the map ends, keep going.

John didn't make it easy to get to him, but boy, he sure could draw a crowd. Once the word spread, streams of people poured into the wilderness looking for the prophet (v. 7). Foot sore, twisting ankles as you trudged along the river bank, about to turn back, you'd pass a group of pilgrims coming the other way, dripping river water and smiling like they'd met the divine. John made it clear to everyone he wasn't Elijah, and he wasn't Messiah, but as God's representatives go, John couldn't be beat, Jesus said to a crowd once (See Matthew 11:11). John was a prophet's prophet, and then some.

Jesus also threw a wink in the direction of John's strange choice of location. Three times Jesus chides the crowd, "What did you go out to see?" (See Matt. 11:7-9.) Then Jesus teases them with some of their own bad assumptions: "A man without a backbone? A man dressed to the nines? A man angling for a seat in the king's cabinet with a guest house on the side of the palace and a member's only key to the royal pool? Who would go into the wilderness to see any of that?!"

John ministered in the wilderness because to receive the ministry John was railing on about, you had to leave your life behind. You had to take the day off from work. You had to clear your calendar. You had to lock up the house, ask the neighbors to feed the dog and bring in the mail. You had to leave the routine in order to hear what you'd been missing. That's what John meant by his thundering, "Repent!" It is a detachment from this world. It is a renouncing of all the things that make us look down, and an embrace of things that make us look up once again. John made people come out to him in the wilderness because the kingdom of God is a coming away from the things of the world that keep us busy and numb, and a pursuit of the things of the next world that make us full and healed and whole.

When John tells his audience, and us along with them, "Prepare the way," this is what he's getting at. "Go back to your old lives," John was saying, "but feel the *oldness* in them. Go back to your lives, but don't fit in them. Go back to your routines, but be hungry for the *more* you can sense hanging just behind the clouds. Let go of this world more and more as you reach for the next. By living toward the kingdom that is coming, you *are* the message of good news and salvation in the midst of all the small

and broken kingdoms of men. People don't need to come out to the wilderness any longer because they can see this *coming away* in you." If John's life is any indication, some people will hate us for dislodging ourselves. Others will be eager to leave the old kingdoms behind, and join us in looking and reaching up.

Faith and Practice: Your life is a battle between kingdoms. What in your life do you need to turn your back on, to walk away from? What from the next life do you need more of? What do you need to walk toward, to reach for, to be full of? Repentance is both a turning *from* and a turning *to*.

Day 14 - Luke 3:1-6
Wilderness, Part 3

The *wilderness* also means to be lost, and unable to arrive at home. This final meaning of wilderness has its origins in Moses and the Exodus. The writer to the Hebrews gives permission to read wilderness in this way: *"For who were those who heard and yet rebelled? Was it not all those who left Egypt led by Moses? And with whom was he provoked for forty years? Was it not with those who sinned, whose bodies fell in the wilderness? And to whom did he swear that they would not enter his rest, but to those who were disobedient? So we see that they were unable to enter because of unbelief"* (Hebrews 3:16-19). In this telling, wilderness is where you are banished if you are locked out of the promised land. It is the opposite of rest. It is a wandering restlessness. It is the perfect description of doubt, denial, disbelief, disobedience.

It's fitting that this is where John unleashes his prophetic announcements. Pouring river water over Jesus himself, John declares to anyone with ears to hear, "If you would be washed, this is he who will do it." (See Mark 1:8.) When John points at Jesus and bellows down his index finger, "Look, there he is! There is the Lamb of God who takes away the sin of the world!" (John 1:29), John is declaring, "Here is the one who clears every blockade and obstacle we throw in his way. Here is the king of mercy and grace barreling down the highway in your direction." By announcing his message in a place like this, John is saying, "Jesus will find you in your doubt, your denial, your disbelief, your disobedience, but don't expect him to leave you stranded in it! The highway (the Gospel of God) that brings him to you is the highway that carries you out with him."

But we are as stubborn, as obstinate, as shifty in our affections as those who provoked God and were left to wander in the wilds for forty years. We turn back. We choose wilderness over rescue again and again. Really, it's a matter of control. Our demand to control our circumstances, our demand to control our outcomes, our demand to control how God must manifest his grace among us—all of these keep us wandering and lost. Control is the one thing we must turn loose to enjoy the fullness of salvation. That's why the return of Jesus is the glorious curtain call of God's salvation. We manage none of it— not the timing of it, not the manner of it, not what it interrupts and renders obsolete. When Jesus comes back, *wilderness* is ended because our control expires. The theological name for this, of course, is *rest*.

Faith and Practice: 1) What do you refuse to relinquish to Jesus? Why exactly? This is wilderness. Can you imagine what rest would feel like and look like here? This is Gospel. 2) What control can you begin to turn loose as a preview of the full *rest* Jesus brings?

WEEK 3
Worship Is Rejoicing in the Promise of Jesus

Zephaniah 3:14-20; Isaiah 12:2-6; Philippians 4:4-7; Luke 3:7-18

Day 15 - Zephaniah 3:14-20

Language of Joy

Singing is the language of joy. It is the dialect the heart that speaks to express exultant celebration. Singing is better than laughter, because it is not only an outburst of joy, but it is a commentary on the cause for it, as well. Singing is a staking of emotional ground and a challenge to any force or power that would try to reclaim it.

As reasons go, joy is one of the better ones Christians have for singing. Singing is also effectively used to incline or direct or vent the heart, as in the singing we might do for reflection and repentance, or in petition and supplication. In this case, the heart is overflowing because its joy can't be bottled up and contained, so there is an eruption, with melody and rhythm propelling it from us.

This prophecy reads like an invitation to the party of all parties, letter pressed on linen paper, and you aren't just invited to attend—you are the guest of honor! All this to-do is being thrown on your account. And of course a fete like this is in order—your scandal has been dismantled! There is no longer any record or recollection of your offense. Your name is spoken lyrically by the host, not through clenched teeth. You are bestowed full rights of membership, and no one will ever have the nerve to ask you to leave or try to escort you off the premises. This reception is for people who do not belong, and they know it, but the host has awarded them his own belonging and they stopped arguing against it ages ago.

So strike up the band and tell them to play all night and into the next day, and the next night after that! Pass the microphone around because the native language at events like this is singing ourselves empty till we've sweated through our tuxes and evening gowns and collapsed on the dance floor and the front of stage breathless and spent. That is, until someone, panting, grabs the mic and calls out, "One more time!" And the band kicks up again, and we all jump back to our feet.

But what assurance do we have that this grand celebration will actually take place? The host is already doing run-throughs with the band... He is already singing his way through the song set (See v. 17)! After all, no one is more overjoyed at what he has done, is doing, and will do for us than he is himself—a people of no standing now wear an otherworldly and unassailable name, a name that is not their own and fully theirs at the same time. If that doesn't call for a show-stopper, nothing does. Soon enough, we'll sing it all together, with the host in our midst, swaying arm-in-arm, singing like there's no tomorrow, because there isn't. All our songs until then are vocal warm-ups.

Faith and Practice: Forget your musical ability (because ability doesn't really matter). What is your disposition and attitude like as you sing? Do you mumble? Stand silent and tight-lipped? Or does the hope of eternity shine into you and come out through your mouth as you sing your part? Move toward this last option, if you don't live there already. (The people around you probably need it too, so don't wait on their approval...)

Day 16 - Zephaniah 3:14-20

Sing for Home

Singing is the soundtrack of home (v. 20). Home is what pulls the tides of harmony and melody from us, along with the lyrics that float on them. But because our home is the salvation of our God, because it is both a condition and a place, an existence we both inhabit and have not yet reached, our songs sound like arrival and longing simultaneously. They ache with a wistful joy.

They are the sound of homecoming and homesick all at the same time. This prophecy inflames the sweet ache of home by reminding us of all the reasons we have to sing.

Of course we sing for home. Home has no judgment (v. 15).
Of course we sing for home. Home has no enemies (v. 15).
Of course we sing for home. Home is where the king dwells (v. 15).
Of course we sing for home. Home has no fear, because it harbors no evil (v. 15).
Of course we sing for home. Home has no weakness, and only victory (v. 16, 17).
Of course we sing for home. Home is furnished with gladness and love (v. 17).
Of course we sing for home. Home is an endless festival and the end of mourning (v. 18).
Of course we sing for home. No reproach or oppressors are welcome here (v. 18, 19).
Of course we sing for home. Home is where the lame dance and the outcast belong (v. 19).
Of course we sing for home. Home has no room for shame. Here, you are dressed in renown (v. 19, 20).
Of course we sing for home. Here, you are gathered, envied, and fortunate (v. 20).
Of course we sing for home…

Faith and Practice: 1) Do you find yourself singing of home often, or rarely? Do you need to adjust this? 2) What's the worst that can happen if you are overheard? 3) What song, hymn, or carol BEST captures your longing for home?

Day 17 - Isaiah 12:2-6

Wolves and Confidence

Isaiah gives us a very fast way to measure our trust in the Savior: how much do you fear? How much are you afraid? The more you fear, the less you trust. The more you trust, the less you fear (v. 2).

An old proverb says, "In every story the wolf comes at last."[3] And that's what sets us to trembling—we are terrified of the wolves the Savior lets slip into our story. They have their function, though, our personal wolves. They are each hand selected and custom made to teach us that God, our Savior, saves us. All the other things we set our confidence in are like wolf bait.

If the Lord is my stronghold and my sure defense, then nothing else can be. Not my finances, not my health and fitness, not my successes, not my standing and reputation, not my intellect, and not my charm. And if it is God who saves me, then surely nothing else will. But I have to learn the failings of each false savior firsthand. I have to be troubled and haunted and hunted. My variety of wolves chase me to each homemade savior in turn, to find that each is flimsy and no defense. Each one must fail to save me so I can abandon them all. Naturally we

---

3 Attributed to the economist Beatrice Webb.

are afraid of the wolves that slip in, or those we invite, but paradoxically, the wolves teach us not to be afraid. The Gospel is a transfer of confidence. It is a joyful loss of confidence in every counterfeit savior we used to cling to and the hard-learned, refitted confidence that Jesus is my sure acceptance. The result of this transfer is fading fear. What is there to be afraid of? Whatever I am given is merely designed to exercise confident faith in the sure Savior. According to the prophecy, this kind of assurance looks like an overflow—rejoicing (v. 3), drinking deep and greedy from the springs of salvation (v. 3), thanksgiving and prayer (v. 4), praise and exaltation (v. 4), missions (v. 4), and a ringing joy (v. 5), until finally faith becomes sight and he is standing in our midst (v. 6). In the meantime, we can give thanks for the wolves, our teachers.

Faith and Practice: What metaphorical wolf has recently caused you to shift your confidence? Because God is saving you, give thanks even for teachers with fangs.

Day 18 - Isaiah 12:2-6

Thirsty

For people who are thirsty, water is a cause for rejoicing. For the thirsty, water is good news. It is relief. On the other hand, it is terrifying and panic-making to run out of water. To experience deep and prolonged thirst is to feel yourself drying out and drying up from the inside. It is a withering, a turning caked and cracked, a going brittle and powdery.

So the metaphor for salvation as a water source, whether a well or bubbling springs, is visceral and gut-level (v. 3). To happen upon a spring in a wild place when in bad need of something to drink is a miraculous, magical experience. Bubbling up, or pouring out from some unseen source, here is what the one who thirsts needs most. For the drinker, the spring seems to be endless, it just trickles, or pours, or flows, as much as required. You can drink until quenched. You can drink past quenched if you like, until it splashes down the front of you and you sit back delirious and water-drunk. For thirsty wanderers or travelers who find a spring, it is healing and reviving. It is a coming-back-to-life. The only adequate way to describe the feeling of all that clean, pure water washing and sloshing through the arid parts of us is *rejoicing*. The satiated bubble over like springs themselves! Just like when the grace of God in Christ first found us and poured over us, or splashed onto us, or washed through us, or bubbled up and ran out of us. However it came, it

doesn't much matter. What matters is the hilarious memory of being the just-thirsty wanderers wiping our mouths at the springs, with Jesus, the great wellspring himself, laughing louder than the lot of us!

God willing, our thirst will never fully leave us in this world. The mystery of it is, the more satisfied we are in Jesus, the more our thirst continues, or even grows. Our thirst now is a holy discontent; it is an annoyance at mouthfuls and swigs and sips. We have had just enough of him to make us crave infinitely more—a state of constant gulps and draughts. Given the nature of deep thirst, when Jesus returns, our reception of him will be like water poured on sand (v. 6).

Faith and Practice: Take a few moments to assess yourself. Are you currently thirsty, or not so much? Can you identify what has piqued your thirst, or dulled it?

Day 19 - Philippians 4:4-7
Telltale Signs

The Lord is near, says Paul, and you announce his proximity with a few telltale signs (v. 5). You are always rejoicing. People roll their eyes at you, you rejoice so much. And you are gentle[4]. With everyone. And you do not worry. Ever. About anything. There is no need. Jesus is in control of all things, and he is constantly dispensing his hilarious reconciliation right through to the climactic end of his unfolding Gospel story. No room for worry. Rejoice, be gentle, don't worry. When these three combine, they create a fourth, exceptionally rare quality: a confounding peace. Like the holy dove itself has roosted in your mind and nested in your heart. If heaven has established unbreakable peace with you through the Son, then you are at peace with the rest of the world in a way that defies all logic.

No wonder no one believes Jesus is near. We don't resemble this at all, most of us.

Let's try on the opposite: Complain, because the Lord is out to frustrate you, and again I say, complain! Be harsh and shrill with everyone, because they probably deserve it. And worry like there's no tomorrow—wring your hands, pull out your hair, sweat bullets, and gnaw the nails off your fingers, because do you really believe that God is at work for you? For others, maybe... but you?! And stir up conflict. Conflict is how we get things done! Conflict is the opposite of good news, but it makes the world go round, if by "go round" you mean "spin out of control." Kicking up conflict will strangle your heart and choke your mind to be sure, but it will strangle and choke everyone else with you.

---

[4] *The common translation here is reasonableness, but gentle is much more vivid and practical. It is also a more accurate proclamation of the Gospel.*

There, that portrait feels more familiar. That fits. And because we look more like these people who are NOT counting on the arrival of a Savior when we speak of the hope of Jesus's return, it is little more than a ghost story.

But do you see what Paul holds out to you if you let go of the familiar and take up the unnatural disposition he profiles at the beginning of these verses? IF you rejoice always, IF you are gentle as a default, IF you shun worry, then you will have peace. Jesus will set up sentries around your heart. And you will have the mind of Christ.

And looking at you, being in your presence, because you no longer resemble anyone from around here, people will sense Jesus is close and drawing closer.

Faith and Practice: 1) Which of these is the truer portrait of you? Rejoicing or complaining? Gentle or rough? Worry or peace? 2) Which of the three—rejoice, be gentle, don't worry—are you going to pursue relentlessly this week? Next week, and the week after, don't forget the others.

Day 20 - Luke 3:7-9

A Newly Planted Garden

John was no serene sage. He was a wild-eyed firebrand. He was more apt to grab his audience by the collars and give them a shake than he was to soothe their spirits. "Why are you here, you knot of snakes?" he'd yell (See v. 7). "What do you want, you slithering hatchlings? A get-out-of-jail-free card? A bit of performative theatre? Or are you here to be turned inside out?" His point was, the kingdom of heaven is only for those who are turned inside out. The kingdom of heaven is not the

sort of thing we can easily fit into our lives, and incorporate into the routine. The kingdom of heaven swallows us whole.

But it's the way that John drops his message that is most discomforting. It's not *what* he says, but *how* he says it. His language reaches all the way back to the garden. "You snakes, did that ancient serpent send you? Have you come out to twist and distort the word of God to your own purposes, too?!" John was just getting warmed up. "Your first parents stole fruit that wasn't theirs—a sacramental sign that God decides what is good and evil from his own character. You are worse! You are an orchard of rotten fruit. You put out whole bumper crops of wrong and falsehood. You deserve the axe and the burn pile!" (See v. 9.)

Now John was on a roll. "And while we're on the subject of trees, don't think your family tree will do you any good, either! Descendants of Abraham, pah! Worthless! Fruitless! Just like your lives. You think God gives a hoot that you can trace your lineage to Abraham? What about your heart? That's what God cares for. Does your heart look like Abraham's? Ready to give up on your own schemes, and designs, and power grabs? Ready to trust God to keep *his* promise in *his* way? Then maybe the axe isn't for you after all; maybe the burn pile doesn't smolder for you. Maybe God will circumcise your heart to match your flesh, cut out the dead part of it and throw it away. Maybe you can be a dead thing made alive, a dull rock turned a true child, a true descendant..." (See v. 8.)

Now John softens as he reaches the finish line. No need to stomp the brokenhearted into the riverbank, after all. "Are you ready to repent? Are you ready to give up on every self-justification? Are you ready to be washed? Then come, and you won't be blighted stalks anymore. You'll be prized fruit trees, putting out the kind of yield that God himself finds sweet."

Snakes turned to saints, trunks to trees, rocks to sons and daughters. The Gospel of God is the same yesterday today, and tomorrow, just like God himself is the same yesterday, today, and tomorrow. Give up on all your conniving and claims of self-provision, and be turned inside out. God is coming to walk in his newly planted garden again, and *you* are the new garden he is planting for himself.

Faith and Practice: Can you look at any part of your life and trace the transformation? Be joyful over it, and give unrestrained thanks to Jesus for working this transformation! Then ask for more, and give unrestrained thanks for that, too.

Day 21 - Luke 3:10-18

Preaching Good News With Money and Material

After John leaned into his audience and called them a serpent's nest, some of his hearers began to writhe and coil in their own skins. "What should we do then? We're sunk for sure" (See v. 10). John's response was as quizzical as ever. "Give away your extra coat, and half your lunch" (v. 11). The tax collectors who had come out to make a holy show started to perspire because they'd made comfortable careers for themselves by *taking* extra, not *giving* it away. "What about us? What do we do?" (v. 12). John told them to collect tax at the legal rate and to stop extorting and grifting the people (v. 13). Enlisted men on leave from the base were next to ask him. "And what about us?" "Same thing," he told them. "No more shakedowns of citizens in back alleys, no more demands for protection money from shopkeepers. You knew the G.I. pay grade when you signed up, so trust God and make a go of it" (v. 14). Ordinary joes, IRS men, and combat veterans all asked John how to be saved, and he told them all that salvation would be found with a lighter wallet.

It wasn't exactly that John was telling them to buy their way into heaven. If John were pulling that kind of con, he'd ask them to become supporters of his ministry, and he'd pocket their donations. But John didn't ask them to give him any money at all. He told them to share. He told them to stop stealing. Somehow, these instructions fit with the rest of his good news sermons. This was how you showed you were washed. This was how you showed the spiritual fruit growing in you from the inside out. This was how you showed you were baptized with the Spirit of grace and love, not the fire of judgment. According to John here, the way you handle money and possessions won't punch your ticket for Kingdom Come, but it bloody well shows whether your ticket is punched.

To this day Christians get slithery as snakes when preachers start to talk about money. Many a camel (See Matthew 19:23-24.) starts to feel pinched and claustrophobic and finds it hard to breathe all of a sudden. Money is the one thing most of us think we need more of in order to be safe and secure and happy and fulfilled. The Gospel has always been consistent on the matter—if the living God has smiled upon you with love, and mercy, and grace, and salvation, money is the last thing you need to worry about. So you can give it away to show you do not trust in your own earning power or portfolio to take care of you, you trust in God alone. Generous hearts are trusting hearts according to the Gospel, and what's more, generous hearts are a chip off the old divine block! All the money in the world won't buy you a single gold brick in the kingdom of heaven, so spend it spiritually while you are here, and spend it all. The best way to prepare for the world to come is to give away the worldly possessions, and concerns, and worries that weigh you down like faithless anchors in this life. Justice and mercy are good news declarations that we stand to receive such a jackpot of an inheritance when the kingdom comes, there is no earthly way to add to it.

Faith and practice: Does the way you use money suggest that you are anchored to this world, or eager for the next?

WEEK 4
The Promise Is Not Finished

Micah 5:2-5a; Psalm 80; Hebrews 10:5-10; Luke 1:39-45 (46-55)

Day 22 - Micah 5:2-5

Most Unlikely

Jesus has always had a thing for the little, the left-out, and the less-than. Probably it's because the strong and self-sufficient and significant don't have much use for him, what with all that strength and self-sufficiency and social standing to fall back on. It was certainly

that way during Micah's time of prophecy. The kings of the northern and southern kingdoms were locked in an arms race, AND they were hell-bent on trying to out-pagan each other, AND somehow they'd taken to eating their subjects and citizens instead of livestock (Micah 3:2, 3)—a Halloween version of Iron Chef. Strength, sufficiency, and significance are often on the hunt for new excesses to indulge.

In ancient days, just as in our own time, the salacious and self-important made sport of stepping on the head of the little guy. Such is the way of the world. It's also the sort of thing prophets loved to denounce most. "In the kingdom of God," they'd bluster, "this power balance will be flipped topsy turvy. The little, and the left-out, and less-than will be seated with God on his throne, and you cannibal kings will be on all fours propping up their feet with your backs!"

That's what makes Bethlehem such an important prophetic and theological site. By choosing Bethlehem as the birthplace for the Davidic king, and the better David to follow, God is signaling to the little, the left-out, and the less-than that he has *us* on his mind and holds *us* in his heart. What he's about to unleash in the world puts *us* first for once.

In all the travel guides of the day, among all the listings of the most notable towns to visit in Samaria and Judea, Bethlehem hardly got a mention. Bethlehem, or *house of bread*, was most famous for its local bakery. Then again, if you've seen one bakery, you've seen them all. According to the reviews, Bethlehem was hardly worth a day trip. Tiny, unimpressive, unimportant, unremarkable Bethlehem was a good place to hail *from* as hardly anyone wanted to hail *to* a hick town like that. In fact, when this part of Micah's prophecy was fulfilled at the birth of Jesus, Herod the Great had to be reminded that there even *was* a prophecy that mentioned Bethlehem at all. God did not need reminding, of course. He'd had Bethlehem set aside for himself all along, just as he'd had the little, the left-out, and the less-than set aside for himself all along.

So in Micah's prophecy, and in the story that unfolds after it, the most unlikely of towns is chosen for the most unlikely of births of the most unlikely of kings, with the most unlikely of reigns and the most unlikely of kingdoms, wielding the most unlikely of salvations for the most unlikely of people.

And it will happen again.

At the most unlikely of times, in the most unlikely of ways, the most unlikely of kings will return to bring the most unlikely of ends of the most unlikely of worlds, while at the same time staging the most unlikely of weddings to the most unlikely of brides.

To be called *most unlikely* in human matters is never a compliment. To be called *most unlikely* in the plan of God's redemption is the same as being called a favorite child.

Faith and Practice: What in your life qualifies you to be called *most unlikely?* Whatever it is, it is not something to be overcome, it is cause for celebration.

Day 23 - Luke 1:46-55

Even Better Than We Dreamed

The title of Mary's song is almost as impossible as the message of the angel, almost as impossible as the promise growing inside her. *Magnificat* is the title the song is known by. It means to *magnify* and it comes from the first verb of the song, *"My soul magnifies the Lord."* It is an impossible title because it's an impossible verb. How do you magnify what doesn't need magnifying in the least? How can you make larger, or more prominent, or more impressive him who is above all things? How can you make greater him who surpasses the greatest greatness? And yet Mary sings the impossible: "Let me add to the name which lacks nothing."

Mary breaks into her magnifying song while cradling her womb and sitting over cups of tea with her cousin Elizabeth at the retirement village. A few days have passed since the angel suddenly stood before her and filled up all the space in her tiny Galilean bedroom so that even the air particles became charged and felt like they were trying to escape. The tiny hairs all over her body are still standing straight out from her skin. Mary has come to stay with Elizabeth for a few months, not to hide away her mistimed pregnancy, but to confirm it. Elizabeth is the custodian of her own prophetic pregnancy, and Mary has come because she believed the angel's strange tidings and wants to believe them even more (See v. 45). The much-too-late nature of Elizabeth's pregnancy proclaims that God has not forgotten his long-coming promise of salvation; the much-too-early nature of Mary's proclaims that this is something entirely new, a divine rebirth for us all.

It's in this parlor scene, as Elizabeth pours more tea, that Mary starts to sing.

> When our God moves near with his salvation
> the lowly are his favorites,
> and the forgotten are renowned (v. 48).
> He is mercy to the spent and used up (v. 50),
> he is the might of the weak (v. 51),
> he is the boast of the humble (v. 52),
> he is the standing and reputation of the no-named (v. 51, 52),
> he is fullness and overflowing for the empty (v. 53),
> and the unbreakable promise who reaches through
> all generations (v.55).

Really, what Mary sings is, "He is even better than we dreamed. Amen." And that is magnification for the one who has no need of it. When greatness stoops down, when greatness reaches out, when greatness pursues, when greatness reconciles and draws us near and holds us close, when greatness shares itself and gives itself to be inhabited and enjoyed, then what cannot be magnified is somehow increased. *"My soul magnifies the Lord,"* Mary sings as Elizabeth sits rocking with her eyes closed and her smiling chin pointing to the ceiling. *"My soul magnifies the Lord."* And because the one she sings for is even better than we dreamed, you'd almost swear it was the Lord who was magnifying Mary's soul (and ours with hers).

Faith and Practice: In your own life, how can you magnify the one beyond magnifying?

Day 24 - Luke 1:44-55

Reminding and Remembering

God doesn't need reminding, but he also doesn't bristle at it, either. There is a long tradition in which God's people replay to him the promises he made to them. In Mary's song she recounts at least a few of them. She sings of God's promise to be Israel's God and Savior (v. 54). She sings of God's promise to give Abraham more children than he could count (v. 55). She sings of God's promise to uphold his own glory through the drama of creation, redemption, and re-creation (v. 50-53). She even sings mention of God's additional promise to use her unprecedented pregnancy to bring all this about (v. 46-49).

God doesn't blush at these reminders because it's not so much that we are calling to mind something he has forgotten, as we are rejoicing with him over what he refuses to forget. In fact, so much of what we do in worship is remembering before him what he has promised:

- In invocations, prayers and hymns, he has promised we always have his ear;
- In baptism, he has promised to pour an oasis into our desert hearts;
- In the sermon, he has promised to never give us the silent treament;
- In confession of sin and assurance of pardon, he has promised to take our offenses personally in order to never take offense at us again;
- In the eucharist, he has promised us a permanent seat at the table;

- In tithes and offerings, he has promised that even if we run low we will never run out;
- In sending us out to minister to the world in his name, he has promised he hasn't lost the fight against the darkness, not by a long-shot, and he isn't finished yet either... and oh yeah, he will never leave us or forsake us.

By reciting and reenacting his promises in all the parts of our worship, what we discover is that there is not a single promise he has defaulted on. By recounting the record day after day, week after week, of divine promises made and kept, shriveled hearts swell with assurance. By recounting his promises and realizing his joy in keeping them all, we are confirmed in the belief that he will keep the final promise as well, and he will send Jesus the groom to collect his unworthy but freely chosen and fully approved bride. By remembering all his promises, privately and corporately, what we discover is that it is not God we are reminding but his wavering saints.

Faith and Practice: Today, what kept promise will you remember before the Lord and be reminded of his faithfulness? Don't forget to remember before him his promise to send Jesus to gather us, and don't forget that this is his only outstanding promise. This should renew your faith and hope in Christ's return.

Day 25 - Psalm 80:1-7
Shepherd

What the world needs most is a shepherd. What the world wants most is just about anything else—a politician who embodies our national idolatries, a celebrity gleaming in the flashbulbs, an athletic hero with a winning record and hall of fame numbers, a social media influencer who parades through pixels modelling the life we crave

for ourselves. All these figures reinforce a myth that's as sweet as a confection: we will prevail. With effort, and talent, and timing, and hard work and career metrics, we can stand on our own. We are the captains of our outcomes.

The presence of a shepherd tells a very different story about who we are. We are lost. We are hunted. We are prey. What story of sheep have you ever heard in which the sheep lead themselves to safety? What sheep have ever steered their own way out of danger? A flock without a shepherd is a buffet for predators.

And so, when some boys from the United Sheep Workers of Bethlehem, Local PS 23, turned up at the manger following the angel-song, it was no accident. They were sent to recognize one of their own, whether or not they recognized it themselves. He was a shepherd just like they were, and at the same time he was more shepherd than they could ever know. Like the best of the trade, he will lead us (v. 1). He will lead us through our tears and out of them (v. 5). He will lead us past our adversaries and swear on his life they can do us no lasting harm (v. 6). He will lead us away from prayers that are selfish and small-hearted and sniveling (v. 4). He will lead us by his own radiance (*"shine forth,"* v. 1), and he will lead us into his glory (*"you who are enthroned upon the cherubim,"* v. 1).

But the kicker is, he will lead us by his beaming smile. Twice it is repeated in our sample of verses (v. 3, 7), three times throughout the entire Psalm. He will lead us for the utter joy he takes in it. He delights in belonging to us, and in us belonging to him. He delights in daring wolves and bears and jackals and rustlers to try and take what's his, grinning wide as a mountain pasture in the knowledge he is an immortal threat to everything that threatens us. He delights in leading us by faith over all the changing face of the terrain and all the way to the last green pasture. He delights in bringing strays close, pulling wandering lambs from their chosen thickets, keeping the herd tight and together. He delights in being all things to the sheep—he is the meadow, he is the brook, he is the fold, he is the path. He delights to be their *home.* There is no safer place for sheep to shelter than under the smile of the shepherd.

And when he comes back, calling for us from the ends of the earth, gathering us in, leading us home, he will come as a shepherd. Of all the titles Jesus wears, Shepherd of Israel may be the most beautiful.

Faith and Practice: In this season of your life, how do you most need a shepherd to lead you? Has he been leading you in a direction that you have resisted? (By the way, have you ever noticed how many hymns cast Jesus in the role of shepherd? That is purposeful.)

Day 26 - Hebrews 10:5-10
The Great Intercession

Empty offerings and sacrifices aren't worth the kindling they are offered up on. Neither is empty worship worth getting out of bed and slumping in the pew for. Mumbled prayers, lethargic eucharists, muttered hymns—the trouble is we have whole lifetimes of empty sacrifices to our credit. Even for the faithful, it is hard to muster all the devotion and will of the heart to heave behind our worship. It is impossible to offer up worship that flies straight and true on the strong wings of need and desire. In the confession of sin found in the Book of Common Prayer, we intone together, "we have not loved you with our whole heart," and even in that repentance we are half-hearted.

The good news for failed worshipers is that Jesus intercedes in all of our worship, every last word and movement and intent of it. What is lacking in our prayers, Jesus fills up with the pleadings of his own undivided heart. Where our singing and liturgy are flat and muted, Jesus always sings and chants like a true king with something to crow about. Where our sacrifices are shoddy and half baked, Jesus tucks them under his perfect and overflowing offerings. When we drop our tithes and gifts in the plate dutifully, but our hearts tighten with the keen awareness that the money could be put to good but less holy use elsewhere, Jesus empties his own pockets with sacred abandon and elation. That is precisely the reason we approach the throne of grace boldly—the flawless worship of Jesus is offered with our names on it, so the empty-handed can waltz in with laughter and rejoicing. There is no room for bargaining or disputing at the throne of grace, only acceptance. Under the high priestly worship of Jesus Christ, the disqualified are wildly approved, and those who brought offerings that don't begin to measure up can trade them in for offerings that break the scales.

If God takes no pleasure in our conniving exercises and theatrics, he is pleased as punch with Jesus the Son. Which means that by trusting and following and depending upon Jesus we become pleasing offerings ourselves. By speaking with Jesus's words, by feeling with his heart, by thinking with his mind, by acting in accord with his ministry, by boasting in his works, by repenting through his cross and resurrection for every botched attempt and every non-attempt, we are the offerings Jesus presents in himself to the Father.

The return of Jesus then will be his final act of intercession. He will come to collect us, to present in his own body a harvest of sanctified hearts and lives—rebels and vandals made lovers and loyalists (See v. 10). As he leads the worship procession through the gates of the New Jerusalem, old instincts will get the better of some of us. More than a few are likely to ask, "But shouldn't we bring with us gifts?" He will answer with messianic mirth, "You *are* the gifts." Once again, the empty-handed are the richest in the kingdom of grace.

Faith and Practice: How would your life change if you trusted in your own offerings less and trusted in the perfect offerings of Jesus more?

Day 27 - Luke 1:39-45
Blessed Are You Anyway

Mary and Elizabeth were not only family, they were a support group. Two women, two prophecies, two pregnancies, both as hard to believe as you please. In both cases, either the cruelty of age or the logic of circumstance undermined the hosting of newborn life. In both cases the women were expecting infants wrapped in scandal or slander. When they embraced, Mary and Elizabeth did not need to whisper to one another, "What will people say?" They knew the score. Folks would draw their own conclusions. They knew the neighbors would talk across backyard fences, the kids on the block would compose limericks about them, the ladies at church would look at them sideways, and the men of town would tell dirty jokes about them down at the tavern. They knew.

So Elizabeth held her young cousin in her arms, and sang, "*Blessed are you anyway.* Because you believed what God has said, blessed are you anyway." Or something like that. That's about the best any of us can ever hope to hear: Blessed are you anyway. There is something in Elizabeth's song that echoes and reverberates in Mary because she sings back, "Blessed am I anyway, blessed are we all anyway, from Abraham down to Mary, down to the next poor sap barely worth a notice in this life, and yet God has reshuffled heaven and earth to enfold him in undying love!" Blessed are you anyway, goes the refrain, and they sang it together until they sang themselves empty.

The next time you are at a dinner party, clink your butter knife on your wine glass. When the guests at the table quiet down and turn to you, say, "Have I mentioned that Jesus *is* coming back?" You *won't* be invited to the next dinner party. You may want to try it anyway because you have nothing to lose but this world. When your friends see you reading a book like this one in the coffee shop, or when they hear and register the lyrics in the hymns on your tongue, or when they see you looking crook-necked past low hanging clouds, they may ask you, "Do you real-

ly believe that? You believe Jesus is coming back?" Do not explain too much. You'll end up explaining the story, and the promise, and the hope away. You really don't have to explain at all. A one-word answer will hold up, even if it feels flimsy in the moment.

Eventually, the impossible pregnancies are delivered. Eventually, the long awaited shepherd/judge/king/groom arrives.

In the meantime, your neighbors will continue to give you pitying half-smiles. Some will give you whole receptions of ridicule and scorn. Mary won't. Elizabeth won't. The remaining, waiting saints won't. The belief that is alive and growing in us will leap for joy at the announcement of yours. Blessed are you anyway.

Faith and Practice: Which do you need more, the approval of friends and family and neighbors, or the return of Jesus? Which do you crave more? The good news is, even when the faith alive in us is embryonic, it can grow and gestate.

Day 28 - Luke 1:(39-45), 46-55
Birth

His second coming will be much like his first. It will be a kind of birth. There is a long, pregnant season of waiting. There is anticipation. There is longing. There is preparation and impatience. There is pain and discomfort before, and joy and relief after. There is inevitability and mystery all at the same time. One moment he will not be with us and the next he will fill up our senses. However he comes, with plumes of flame like a rocket falling to earth, or riding a flying carpet made of cumulus and nimbus, or slipping between the atoms to stand among us as easily as we step from one room into the next, he will enter our lives more fully, more entirely. He will command all our attention and energy and time. In these ways, his coming is another birth.

> And because he comes to be the strength that scatters our oppressors (v.51);
> Because he comes to throw down tyrants from their thrones, and seat us with him on his (v. 52);
> Because he comes to fill all our hungering aches (v. 53);
> And make us rich in ways we can't compute(v. 53, 54);
> Because he comes to relieve and defend his servants against every hurt (v. 51);
> Because he comes as a promise made, remembered constantly, guarded and now kept (v. 55);
> Because he comes as Abraham's wildest dream and teary-eyed hope (v.55);
> Because he comes to uphold eternity (v. 55);
> Because he comes as our unending *Amen*.

Because of all this, his second coming will be much like his first. It will be a kind of birth, but the ones being born and un-wombed to life are ourselves.

Faith and Practice: Before birth, infants kick and thrash in the womb. What holy kicks do you notice in yourself? What holy kicks would you like to notice more of?

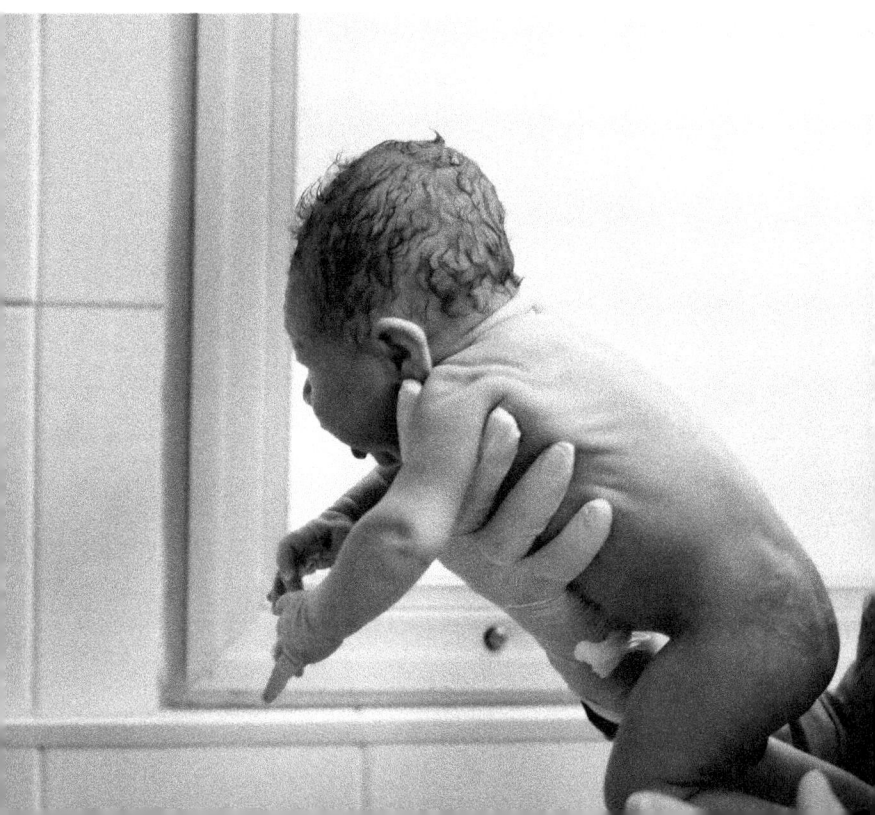

Notes

Notes

Awaken the awe and wonder of Advent.

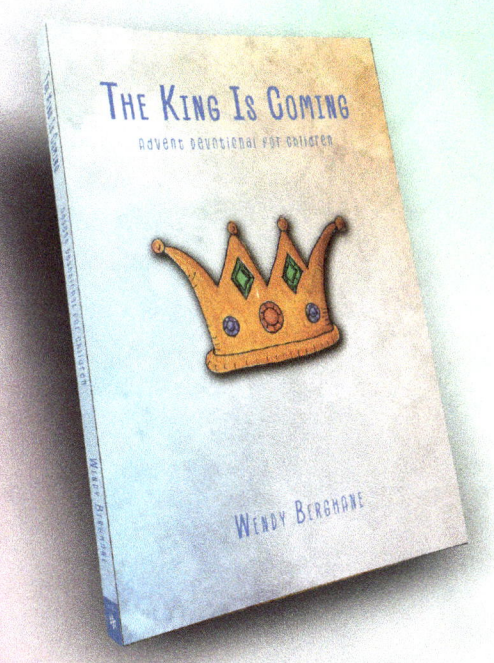

Bring your family together this Advent season for a journey exploring God's big love for you! *The King is Coming* is full of fun, meaningful, hands-on activities, sure to reach young hearts!

iblestudymedia.com   info@biblestudymedia.com

More cups for thirsty souls.

THE CHRISTIAN LIFE TRILOGY
The Crucified Life
The Resurrected Life
The Spirit-Filled Life

DRAW NEAR

A LIVING HOPE

WALKING IN LIGHT

TRUSTING GOD

THE CROSS WALK

HEARTS ALIVE SERIES
Children's Church
Fall
Winter
Spring
Summer

HEARTS ALIVE SERIES
Sunday School
Fall
Winter
Spring

Bible Study Media
Igniting Hearts. Engaging Minds.

biblestudymedia.com

Bible study reimagined.

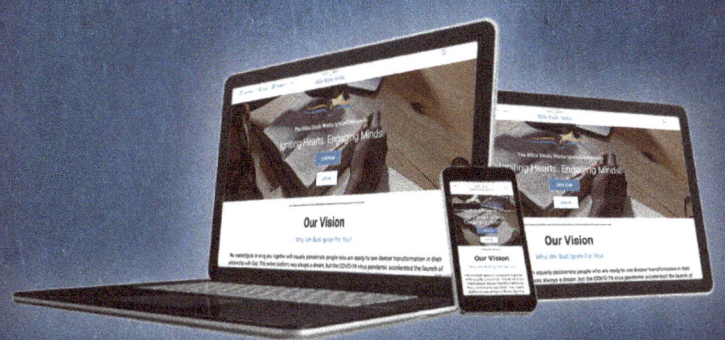

Introducing an online comunity at ignite.biblestudymedia.com.

Ignite was created so that you can study the Bible at any time, in any place, with a global community of believers. **Connect today.**

Bible Study Media
Igniting Hearts. Engaging Minds.

www.ingramcontent.com/pod-product-compliance
Lightning Source LLC
Chambersburg PA
CBHW041131110526
44592CB00020B/2763